AF486485

Poems for the Christian Heart

by

Stephen Baley

Poems for the Christian Heart

Written by Stephen Baley

Edited by Stephen Baley

Published by Stephen Baley

Cover Design by Stephen Baley

Interior Design Stephen Baley

© 2023 Stephen Baley

All images from public domain.

All Scripture is used from the Holy Bible.

For questions, comments, concerns, requests, or speaking engagements, see *Stay in Touch*.

Table of Contents

Introduction

Dear reader, welcome to *Poems for the Christian Heart*. In this book of poems, we explore the deep chambers of the soul and the innermost yearnings of the Christian heart. Be it passions such as anger and jealousy, the eternally abounding mercy and grace of God, or heaven, the lake of fire, and eternity, these thirty-one poems will walk with you through some of the most intense wars humans ever fight within their being and wrestle with you through deep theology.

This poetic book seeks to comfort you in the darkest of days, encourage you when all hope seems lost, and grow you when the time to rise to the challenge is upon you. Be it proclaiming the Gospel, calling men to repentance, or loving your enemies, you will encounter various spiritual challenges throughout this book whose desire is to mold you into the image of our beloved Lord Jesus Christ and draw you to Him.

Poems for the Christian Heart does not shy away from the difficult truths of the Scriptures yet still seeks to bring you motivation, encouragement, and bright hope through reminding you of the promises of the Lord. Whatever circumstances may be occurring in your life, this book likely touches upon that topic in one of its many poems. So, take a moment out of your hectic day, grab a pen for reflective notes, and read the poem that applies to what it is you are going through today. I pray that the Lord will grow you, shape you, encourage you, discipline you, and maybe even save you through *Poems for the Christian Heart.*

Day 1

Forever

Even before the world began,
He chose me by His sovereign hand

He picked me up in my despair,
And appointed me His righteous heir

From the lake of fire He has saved me
To be with Him throughout eternity

Never again will I be alone,
For my sins, He has atoned

I have been bought with the blood of the Lamb
And am forever a child of the Great I Am

With my Savior I will always be
To behold His face to forever see

What is this grace that He should die for me
So He could receive me with unending glee?

What joy shall fill me on that great and fateful day
When I behold Him who was with me all the way

To be with Him and His children I will forever be
In the place in which there is no more sea

But between now and then I shall live for the Lord
To bring glory to God by the blade of His sword

To continue to serve Him after my time is done
To do His will, to the glory of the Son

Amen

"…just as He chose us in Him before the foundation of the world, that we would be holy and blameless before Him. In love He predestined us to adoption as sons through Jesus Christ to Himself, according to the kind intention of His will, to the praise of the glory of His grace, which He freely bestowed on us in the Beloved."

Ephesians 1:4-6 NASB1995

"Jesus said to her, 'I am the resurrection and the life; he who believes in Me will live even if he dies, and everyone who lives and believes in Me will

*never die. Do you believe this?' She *said to Him, 'Yes, Lord; I have believed that You are the Christ, the Son of God, even He who comes into the world.'"*

John 11:25-27 NASB1995

"There will no longer be any curse; and the throne of God and of the Lamb will be in it, and His bond-servants will serve Him; they will see His face, and His name will be on their foreheads. And there will no longer be any night; and they will not have need of the light of a lamp nor the light of the sun, because the Lord God will illumine them; and they will reign forever and ever."

Revelation 22:3-5 NASB1995

Reflective Notes:

Day 2

<u>Who Is This?</u>

Who is this great and mighty King
Of whom the saints and angels sing?

Who is He who put the stars in place
Who saved His children by His grace?

Who is this who commands planets where to orbit
Who rules from His throne on high on which He sits?

Who is this who makes demons shudder
Who apart from Him there is no other?

Who is this who tells the oceans how far to rise

Yet we cannot see with our earthly eyes?

This is Jesus, this is He
Who one day all will see

He shall return on His white horse
To set His enemies on their course

In the lake of fire they will be
For His chosen ones to always see

To gaze upon their everlasting suffering
Because of their rejection of the One, True King

Praise be to the God of all creation
Who sends His foes to everlasting damnation!

For the wrath of God will forever be
With those who reject Him everlastingly

This God of the heavens they have denied
And they shall die for their stubborn pride

The Lord of great glories they have rejected
Always and forever they will be dejected

This is Jesus, the One worthy of glory and praise
To Him our anthem we shall forever raise

Live for Him the rest of your life
To the day there shall be no more strife

Yes, this is Jesus, this is He.

This is Jesus, for all eternity.

"Lift up your heads, O gates,
And be lifted up, O ancient doors,
That the King of glory may come in!
Who is the King of glory?
The Lord strong and mighty,
The Lord mighty in battle.
Lift up your heads, O gates,
And lift them up, O ancient doors,
That the King of glory may come in!
Who is this King of glory?
The Lord of hosts,
He is the King of glory. Selah."

Psalm 24:7-10 NASB1995

"Safe? Who said anything about safe? 'Course he isn't safe. But he's good. He's the King, I tell you."

-Mr. Beaver to Lucy regarding Aslan

Reflective Notes:

Day 3

Let It Go

What worry troubles your heart today
Concerning which you need to pray?
Take it to Jesus, and let it go.

What stress worries your soul
Which on you takes its toll?
Take it to Jesus, and let it go.

Take it to Jesus, for He is always there.
No matter what, go to Him in prayer.

Stay faithful to Him who is faithful to you
And watch His promises always come true

He is there to rescue those who draw near to Him
And are faithful to repent of their dreadful sin

Look at how much He did on the cross
So you and I would not be at loss

Your everlasting soul you have trusted Him to save
So why should faith in Him ever, ever cave?

He rose from the grave and defeated your sin
So at what can we not look, and grin?

He has given His elect everlasting life
So why in our hearts should there ever be strife?

What worries trouble your heart today
Concerning which you need to pray?
Take it to Jesus, and let it go.

What worry troubles your soul
which on you takes its toll?
Take it to Jesus, and let it go.

Let it go, let it go…

"Rejoice in the Lord always; again I will say, rejoice! Let your gentle spirit be known to all men. The Lord is near. Be anxious for nothing, but in everything by prayer and supplication with thanksgiving let your requests be made known to God. And the peace of God, which surpasses all comprehension, will guard your hearts and your minds in Christ Jesus. Finally, brethren, whatever is

true, whatever is honorable, whatever is right, whatever is pure, whatever is lovely, whatever is of good repute, if there is any excellence and if anything worthy of praise, dwell on these things. The things you have learned and received and heard and seen in me, practice these things, and the God of peace will be with you."

Philippians 4:4-9 NASB1995

"Therefore humble yourselves under the mighty hand of God, that He may exalt you at the proper time, casting all your anxiety on Him, because He cares for you."

1 Peter 5:6-7 NASB1995

Reflective Notes:

Day 4

<u>*Key*</u>

The love of God is the key to all life.
The love of God gives everlasting life.

To those who call on His name and repent of their sin
He draws to Himself and welcomes them in

Because of His love, He chose us in Him
Even before the world could begin

In eternity past He had already chosen
Those who would be His beloved children

Without His love there would be no hope
Without which we could in no way cope

Dead men we were before His love came in
And changed us forever to be born again

Because of His sovereign grace
We shall see Him face to face

With all of our fellow Christians
We shall worship He who is risen

Take joy in Him, all you who are His!
For because of Him, you will always have bliss!

Always and forever you shall always be
With the One who died for you and for me

Praise be to God for His endless love
Which is as gentle as a delicate dove

Because of His love, He paid a great cost
So that we would not be forever lost

For the love of God is the key to all life
For the love of God gives everlasting life

"For God so loved the world, that He gave His only begotten Son, that whoever believes in Him shall not perish, but have eternal life. For God did not send the Son into the world to judge the world, but that the world might be saved through Him."

John 3:16-17 NASB1995

"Beloved, let us love one another, for love is from

God; and everyone who loves is born of God and knows God. The one who does not love does not know God, for God is love. By this the love of God was manifested in us, that God has sent His only begotten Son into the world so that we might live through Him. In this is love, not that we loved God, but that He loved us and sent His Son to be the propitiation for our sins."

1 John 4:7-10 NASB1995

Reflective Notes:

Day 5

Wrath

The wrath of God is to be greatly feared
By all those who refuse to draw near

The anger of the Lord will consume His enemies
And inflict pain upon all their extremities

For the worm will forever feast on their flesh
For their meat shall always be fresh

There will be no escape from that everlasting fire
No matter how much they deeply desire

For new bodies they shall be given
By Him they rejected yet is risen

Tortured forever they shall be

By the Lamb they'll dread to see

Physical and mental suffering they shall endure
And be worse off than the worst of manure

Emotional and spiritual suffering they too shall bear
For anguish and turmoil shall always be their snare

With their spines ever-bending
Their torture shall have no ending

Their punishment shall be seen by all the righteous
Who trust in Him and delight in His goodness

Praise the Lord, who saved us from the ceaseless fire
With whom we'll always be, the One our souls desire

"Many of those who sleep in the dust of the ground will awake, these to everlasting life, but the others to disgrace and everlasting contempt."

Daniel 12:2 NASB1995

"Then death and Hades were thrown into the lake of fire. This is the second death, the lake of fire. And if anyone's name was not found written in the book of life, he was thrown into the lake of fire."

Revelation 20:14-15 NASB1995

"And David says, 'Let their table become a snare and a trap, and a stumbling block and a retribution to them. Let their eyes be darkened to see not, and

bend their backs forever.”

Romans 11:9-10 NASB1995

“If your eye causes you to stumble, throw it out; it is better for you to enter the kingdom of God with one eye, than, having two eyes, to be cast into hell, where their worm does not die, and the fire is not quenched.”

Mark 9:47-48 NASB1995

Reflective Notes:

Day 6

<u>Heaven</u>

The fellowship of heaven, how sweet it must be
To dwell in such joy, throughout eternity

To forever embrace those for whom your soul longs
In whose presence you break out in joyful song

To hold those closely you hold near and dear
Who losing them is something to never fear

For those who have been captured by their Delight,
Never again will they experience fright

To dance in the heavens with the family of God
And on the street of gold to forever trod

With all the saints of all the ages
To live all the days as written on His pages

To partake in the fruit of the heavenly gardens
Because forever our sin He has pardoned

To live with the Father, the Son, and the Spirit
In that glorious city and all who dwell in it

To everlastingly be with the Lamb who was slain
Who through His suffering spared us fiery pain

The hope of heaven is upon all who trust in the Lord
For they shall be spared from the Son and His sword

They shall dwell with Him for the rest of eternity
with His angels and saints, with you and with me

*"I say to you that many will come from east and
west, and recline at the table with Abraham, Isaac,
and Jacob in the kingdom of heaven."*

Matthew 8:11 NASB1995

*"The Lord of hosts will prepare a lavish banquet for
all peoples on this mountain; a banquet of aged
wine, choice pieces with marrow, and refined, aged
wine. And on this mountain He will swallow up the
covering which is over all peoples, even the veil
which is stretched over all nations. He will swallow
up death for all time, and the Lord God will wipe
tears away from all faces, and He will remove the
reproach of His people from all the earth; for the*

Lord has spoken. And it will be said in that day, 'Behold, this is our God for whom we have waited that He might save us. This is the Lord for whom we have waited; let us rejoice and be glad in His salvation.'"

Isaiah 25:6-9 NASB1995

"But that the dead are raised, even Moses showed, in the passage about the burning bush, where he calls the Lord the God of Abraham, and the God of Isaac, and the God of Jacob. Now He is not the God of the dead but of the living; for all live to Him."

Luke 20:37-38 NASB1995

Reflective Notes:

Day 7

Peace

Apart from God, what hope does man possess?
For even his own soul, he cannot caress.

Though momentary comfort he may shortly bring
In the end, there is nothing to which to cling

Upon his deathbed there will be no lasting peace
For apart from God, his pain will never cease

For unless He repents and trusts in the Lord,
He'll have nothing from Him but His holy sword

To you who read this, repent if you are able
Lest "smitten of God" forever be your label

Put your faith in Jesus for salvation
Trusting that He's your propitiation

You'll be forgiven of all your sin

And be given Christ to dwell within

Live for Him the rest of your days
Until you go home to sing His praise

Have faith in Him throughout your life
And in every moment in which there's strife

In your most private of moments, in your darkest hour
Cry out to Him, and behold His power

Submit yourself to Him
And surrender all your sin

Be at peace with God above
Being forever in His love

"The steadfast of mind You will keep in perfect peace, because he trusts in You. Trust in the Lord forever, for in God the Lord, we have an everlasting Rock."

Isaiah 26:3-4 NASB1995

"Therefore, having been justified by faith, we have peace with God through our Lord Jesus Christ..."

Romans 5:1 NASB1995

"Peace I leave with you; My peace I give to you; not as the world gives do I give to you. Do not let your heart be troubled, nor let it be fearful."
John 14:27 NASB1995

"Let the peace of Christ rule in your hearts, to which indeed you were called in one body; and be thankful. Let the word of Christ richly dwell within you, with all wisdom teaching and admonishing one another with psalms and hymns and spiritual songs, singing with thankfulness in your hearts to God."

Colossians 3:15-16 NASB1995

Reflective Notes:

Day 8

<u>Loneliness</u>

Loneliness, the enemy of all mankind
For it makes life an arduous grind

No companionship is a weight on a man's heart
How he desires for friends to never depart!

What is the solution for such a weighty matter?
How does one deal with such a disaster?

Isolation is felt deep to the bones
And can make a man dreadfully groan

It leads him to yearn for heaven above
For the land with unending love

To forever be with the holy Trinity
And always with His loving family

But between now and then we shall be with them here
And always draw close to those we hold dear

In the hopes of being with them throughout eternity
To forever dwell with them in God's holy city

This is the hope that keeps men going
When their loneliness they are loathing

Is loneliness your ever-present enemy too?
Is it something without which you could do?

Seek out and find fellowship with His sheep
For your sanity and peace to hopefully keep

Find those who accept you as you are
And help you with your inner scars

Find those who preach the Bible
And whose study is not idle

Pray to Him for a faithful church to find
In which your loneliness can take a recline

Love and serve the church with all you are
Serving her both near and far

Go not just for companionship but to minister too
Your ultimate purpose do not misconstrue

Preach the Gospel, call men to repentance,
And makes disciples with every sentence

Go and serve the Lord and His wife
With humble heart, with all of your life

Though it can be hard to find a biblical church
Do not give up on this holy search

Though it can be lonely in your time here
There is no need to forever fear

There is a home far above the stars
In which there are no more scars

But between now and then, obey Hebrews 10:25
Both now and forever, with His children strive

Amen

"Let us hold fast the confession of our hope without wavering, for He who promised is faithful; and let us consider how to stimulate one another to love and good deeds, not forsaking our own assembling together, as is the habit of some, but encouraging one another; and all the more as you see the day drawing near."

Hebrews 10:23-25 NASB1995

"Then the Lord God said, 'It is not good for the man to be alone; I will make him a helper suitable for him.'"

Genesis 2:18 NASB1995

"Two are better than one because they have a good return for their labor. For if either of them falls, the one will lift up his companion. But woe to the one who falls when there is not another to lift him up. Furthermore, if two lie down together they keep warm, but how can one be warm alone? And if one can overpower him who is alone, two can resist him. A cord of three strands is not quickly torn apart."

Ecclesiastes 4:9-12 NASB1995

Reflective Notes:

Day 9

<u>Anger</u>

Anger is one that causes deep scars
When words are spewed and taken to far

It is one that cuts deep to the core
And makes one's soul deeply sore

With unbridled anger, a fire can rage
And cause many a man to disengage

In moments of rage, watch what you say
Before you speak, remember to pray

Though righteous anger is of the Lord

Make sure you're biblical before using the sword

Let all you say be out of concern
Be careful of bridges you may burn

Though there are those that need to be ash
Inquire of the Lord before you slash

Let your tongue be not for evil, but only for good
So when it comes to die, you did all you could

To speak the truth in love
Being gentle as a dove

So be careful of what you speak
And let not sinful rage peak

For anger is one that causes deep scars
When words are spewed and taken to far

It is one that cuts deep to the core
And makes one's soul deeply sore

"A gentle answer turns away wrath, but a harsh word stirs up anger. The tongue of the wise makes knowledge acceptable, but the mouth of fools spouts folly. The eyes of the Lord are in every place, watching the evil and the good. A soothing tongue is a tree of life, but perversion in it crushes the spirit."

Proverbs 15:1-4 NASB1995

"This you know, my beloved brethren. But everyone

must be quick to hear, slow to speak, and slow to anger; for the anger of man does not achieve the righteousness of God. Therefore, putting aside all filthiness and all that remains of wickedness, in humility receive the word implanted, which is able to save your souls. But prove yourselves doers of the word, and not merely hearers who delude themselves For if anyone is a hearer of the word and not a doer, he is like a man who looks at his natural face in a mirror; for once he has looked at himself and gone away, he has immediately forgotten what kind of person he was. But one who looks intently at the perfect law, the law of liberty, and abides by it, not having become a forgetful hearer but an effectual doer, this man will be blessed in what he does.

If anyone thinks himself to be religious, and yet does not bridle his tongue but deceives his own heart, this man's religion is worthless. Pure and undefiled religion in the sight of our God and Father is this: to visit orphans and widows in their distress, and to keep oneself unstained by the world."

James 1:19-27 NASB1995

"And the tongue is a fire, the very world of iniquity; the tongue is set among our members as that which defiles the entire body, and sets on fire the course of our life, and is set on fire by hell."

James 3:6 NASB1995

Reflective Notes:

Day 10

Jealousy

Beware of jealousy, for it can poison your heart
If you find it within, quickly from it depart!

Be grateful for what you have been given
For you have the One who has been risen

Everlasting life you will always possess
So what jealousy do you need to address?

Do you desire the things of your neighbor
Forgetting what you have of your Creator?

Every good gift is from above
Coming down from the Father of love

What each is given is His own choice
So why against He should we raise our voice?

Are His ways not faithful and true?
Does He His gifts misconstrue?

Is the Lord of all not just and good?
He who in your place willingly stood

If you have trusted in Him for salvation
And trust that He is your propitiation?

Then be grateful for what you have been given
For you have the One who is forever risen

"Make sure that your character is free from the love of money, being content with what you have; for He Himself has said, 'I will never desert you, nor will I ever forsake you,' so that we confidently say, 'The Lord is my helper, I will not be afraid. What will man do to me?'"

Hebrews 13:5-6 NASB1995

"See that no one repays another with evil for evil, but always seek after that which is good for one another and for all people. Rejoice always; pray without ceasing; in everything give thanks; for this is God's will for you in Christ Jesus."

1 Thessalonians 5:15-18 NASB1995

"Do not be deceived, my beloved brethren. Every good thing given and every perfect gift is from above, coming down from the Father of lights, with whom there is no variation or shifting shadow."

James 1:16-17 NASB1995

"What then shall we say to these things? If God is for us, who is against us? He who did not spare His own Son, but delivered Him over for us all, how will He not also with Him freely give us all things?

Romans 8:31-32 NASB1995

Reflective Notes:

Day 11

Righteous Revenge

Are you deeply bitter with your neighbor?
Do you wish to strike him with a saber?

Did he bring you harm or mar your name
Or bring your reputation to lasting shame?

Does he lead your soul to be restless at night?
In his destruction would you take delight?

As tempting as it may be
To destroy him with much glee

Pray to the Lord for his soul to be saved
Trusting He'll deal with how he behaved

Either his sin was paid for at Calvary

Or he will suffer throughout eternity

But love him for now, from here to the end
And maybe one day, he will call you friend

Remember when you were an enemy of the cross
And would have suffered everlasting loss

Had Christ not stepped in and bought your salvation
And saved you forever from certain damnation

With the love God has shown you, His former enemy
Show also to everyone, and do so with glee

Trusting one day His revenge will be brought about
To which all His saints will give joyful shout

*"For while we were still helpless, at the right
time Christ died for the ungodly. For one will hardly
die for a righteous man; though perhaps for the
good man someone would dare even to die. But
God demonstrates His own love toward us, in that
while we were yet sinners, Christ died for us. Much
more then, having now been justified by His blood,
we shall be saved from the wrath of God through
Him. For if while we were enemies we were
reconciled to God through the death of His Son,
much more, having been reconciled, we shall be
saved by His life. And not only this, but we also
exult in God through our Lord Jesus Christ,
through whom we have now received the
reconciliation."*

Romans 5:6-11 NASB1995

"You have heard that it was said, 'You shall love your neighbor and hate your enemy.' But I say to you, love your enemies and pray for those who persecute you, so that you may be sons of your Father who is in heaven; for He causes His sun to rise on the evil and the good, and sends rain on the righteous and the unrighteous."

Matthew 5:43-45 NASB1995

"Never pay back evil for evil to anyone. Respect what is right in the sight of all men. If possible, so far as it depends on you, be at peace with all men. Never take your own revenge, beloved, but leave room for the wrath of God, for it is written, 'VENGEANCE IS MINE, I WILL REPAY,' says the Lord. 'BUT IF YOUR ENEMY IS HUNGRY, FEED HIM, AND IF HE IS THIRSTY, GIVE HIM A DRINK; FOR IN SO DOING YOU WILL HEAP BURNING COALS ON HIS HEAD.' Do not be overcome by evil, but overcome evil with good."

Romans 12:17-21 NASB1995

"If possible, so far as it depends on you, be at peace with all men. Never take your own revenge, beloved, but leave room for the wrath of God, for it is written, 'Vengeance is Mine, I will repay,' says the Lord. 'But if your enemy is hungry, feed him, and if he is thirsty, give him a drink; for in so doing you will

"For after all it is only just for God to repay with affliction those who afflict you, and to give relief to you who are afflicted and to us as well when the Lord Jesus will be revealed from heaven with His mighty angels in flaming fire, dealing out retribution to those who do not know God and to those who do not obey the gospel of our Lord Jesus. These will pay the penalty of eternal destruction, away from the presence of the Lord and from the glory of His power, when He comes to be glorified in His saints on that day, and to be marveled at among all who have believed—for our testimony to you was believed."

2 Thessalonians 1:6-10 NASB1995

"'For behold, the day is coming, burning like a furnace; and all the arrogant and every evildoer will be chaff; and the day that is coming will set them ablaze,' says the Lord of hosts, 'so that it will leave them neither root nor branch. But for you who fear My name, the sun of righteousness will rise with healing in its wings; and you will go forth and skip about like calves from the stall. You will tread down the wicked, for they will be ashes under the soles of your feet on the day which I am preparing,' says the Lord of hosts."

Malachi 4:1-3 NASB1995

"And the sea gave up the dead which were in it, and death and Hades gave up the dead which were in them; and they were judged, every one of them

according to their deeds. Then death and Hades were thrown into the lake of fire. This is the second death, the lake of fire. And if anyone's name was not found written in the book of life, he was thrown into the lake of fire."

Revelation 20:13-15 NASB1995

Reflective Notes:

Day 12

Brevity

The brevity of life, how incredibly short
It won't be long before we all report

To the throne of the Lord Almighty
To give an account for all to see

Of how we lived for heaven's purpose
Or if our lives were a three-ring circus

Filled with chasing silly things
Of which eternity does not ring

Your life will be measured compared to His desire
And what is not worthy will be burned with fire

For those who reject the Lord and His Son
Forever they'll burn, their relief will be none

But for those who are His they shall forever be
With the King and His Son, throughout eternity

But between now and then when you leave this earth
How will you live with your second birth?

Live for the Lord while you still have time
For your life could change, right on a dime

For it won't be long before you're at heaven's door
To forever with the angels always soar

Live for Him for the rest of your earthly days
For the King of glory, on whom you'll gaze

To always live before His holy face
Your life's work done, in His embrace

*"Yet you do not know what your life will be like
tomorrow. You are just a vapor that appears for a
little while and then vanishes away."*

James 5:14 NASB1995

*"According to the grace of God which was given to
me, like a wise master builder I laid a foundation,
and another is building on it. But each man must be*

*careful how he builds on it. For no man can lay
a foundation other than the one which is laid, which
is Jesus Christ.*

*Now if any man builds on the foundation with gold,
silver, precious stones, wood, hay, straw, each man's
work will become evident; for the day will show it
because it is to be revealed with fire, and the fire
itself will test the quality of each man's work. If any
man's work which he has built on it remains, he
will receive a reward. If any man's work is burned
up, he will suffer loss; but he himself will be saved,
yet so as through fire."*

1 Corinthians 3:10-15 NASB1995

*"A voice is calling, 'Clear the way for the Lord in
the wilderness; make smooth in the desert a
highway for our God. Let every valley be lifted up,
and every mountain and hill be made low; and let
the rough ground become a plain, and the rugged
terrain a broad valley; then the glory of the Lord
will be revealed, and all flesh will see it together; for
the mouth of the Lord has spoken.' A voice says,
'Call out.' Then he answered, 'What shall I call
out?' All flesh is grass, and all its loveliness is like
the flower of the field. The grass withers, the flower
fades, when the breath of the Lord blows upon it;
surely the people are grass. The grass withers, the
flower fades, but the word of our God stands
forever."*

Isaiah 40:3-8 NASB1995

Reflective Notes:

Day 13

<u>Praise be to the Lord!</u>

Praise be to the Lord!

Praise be to the Lord, the God of all the earth!
Praise be to the Lord, who gave us second birth!

Praise be to the Lord, who gave so He could redeem!
Praise be to the Lord, whose grace is a lasting stream!

Praise be to the Lord, who never leaves His children!
Praise be to the Lord, who forgives them all their sin!

Praise be to the Lord, the great heavenly Host!
Praise be to the Lord, of whom we'll always boast!

Praise be to the Lord!

"Praise the LORD!
Praise God in His sanctuary;
Praise Him in His mighty expanse.
Praise Him for His mighty deeds;
Praise Him according to His excellent greatness.
Praise Him with trumpet sound;
Praise Him with harp and lyre.
Praise Him with timbrel and dancing;
Praise Him with stringed instruments and pipe.
Praise Him with loud cymbals;
Praise Him with resounding cymbals.
Let everything that has breath praise the LORD.
Praise the LORD!"

Psalm 151:1-6 NASB1995

"I will bless the Lord at all times;
His praise shall continually be in my mouth.
My soul will make its boast in the Lord;
The humble will hear it and rejoice.
O magnify the Lord with me,
And let us exalt His name together."

Psalm 34:1-3 NASB1995

"And the four living creatures, each one of them
having six wings, are full of eyes around and
within; and day and night they do not cease to say,
'Holy, holy, holy is the Lord God, the Almighty, who
was and who is and who is to come.' And when the
living creatures give glory and honor and thanks to
Him who sits on the throne, to Him who lives
forever and ever, the twenty-four elders will fall

down before Him who sits on the throne, and will worship Him who lives forever and ever, and will cast their crowns before the throne, saying, 'Worthy are You, our Lord and our God, to receive glory and honor and power; for You created all things, and because of Your will they existed, and were created.'"

Revelation 4:8-11 NASB1995

Reflective Notes:

Day 14

Conductor

Christ the Lord, the great Conductor!
Christ the Lord, the great Sustainer!

Every bird, every fish, every bug, every beast,
He rules them all, from the greatest to the least

Every star in the sky to every grain of sand
He rules them all by His righteous right hand

Every inch of the universe is under His control
Underneath His ruling where there is no lull

Christ the Lord, who died on the cross

Is the One who prevents lasting loss

His sheer willpower holds all that is in existence
And it will always do so, with eternal persistence

Christ the Lord, the great Conductor!
Christ the Lord, the great Sustainer!

"For by Him all things were created, both in the heavens and on earth, visible and invisible, whether thrones or dominions or rulers or authorities—all things have been created through Him and for Him. He is before all things, and in Him all things hold together."

Colossians 1:16-17 NASB1995

Reflective Notes:

Day 15

Christmas

The birth of the Savior that fateful day
Born to take much sin away

Laying in the manger was the God of creation
Who was born to die for man's salvation

The shepherds left their sheep they watched by night
to see the Lord incarnate, O' what a sight!

They beheld the Savior in the virgin's arms
Within there was peace, and no alarm

For the Savior came from heaven above
To save the shepherds by perfect love

The wisemen came because of His presence
To bring Him gold, myrrh, and frankincense

The wisemen knew from the prophets of old
That this was the Savior of which time had told

This little baby in the manger
Would grow to be in danger

To be slain by the One who sent Him from on high
And for the one who birthed him to watch Him die

Weep she would for the slaughtering of her son
As the evil ones believed they indeed had won

But on the third day He would rise again
To prove to all He has defeated sin

The baby in the manger is now King on the throne
Through His work, He has reaped what was sown

Now God has exalted Him to the second highest place
For all to see Him and to behold His face

His mother who held him that fateful day
Is now held by Him, forever to stay

The question for you is, dear reader,
Do you know your Creator?

Have you trusted the baby in the manger
Who is the one and only Savior?

Have you repented of all your sin?
Does the Holy Spirit dwell within?

Submit your life in service to Him
To He who died and rose again

Call on Him to save you today
So in His arms you can forever stay

Celebrate Christmas with the sheep of the Savior
Become part of the fold and with us forever

Christmas is everyday for the children of the King
For always and forever Christmas bells shall ring

The Reason for the season is why His sheep can't die
So come join us forever in the sweet by and by

In the hope of seeing you there,
For you I will say a prayer

That you'll one day know the Savior
And be with His sheep forever

In unending celebration of Christmas Day
With the One who takes their sins away

With the family of God, they shall always be
Now, forever, and throughout eternity

Merry Christmas to you who reads this
I pray to see you in unending bliss

With the King of Christmas and His many sheep
Whom are all the souls He shall forever keep

The birth of the Savior that fateful day
Born to take much sin away

Laying in the manger was the God of all creation
Who was born to die for man's salvation

*"She will bear a Son; and you shall call His name
Jesus, for He will save His people from their sins."*

Matthew 1:21 NASB1995

*"'Come now, and let us reason together,' says
the LORD, 'Though your sins are as scarlet, they will
be as white as snow; though they are red like
crimson, they will be like wool. If you consent and
obey, you will eat the best of the land; but if you
refuse and rebel, you will be devoured by the sword.'
Truly, the mouth of the LORD has spoken."*

Isaiah 40:18-20 NASB1995

*"For God so loved the world, that He gave His only
begotten Son, that whoever believes in Him shall not
perish, but have eternal life. For God did not send
the Son into the world to judge the world, but that
the world might be saved through Him."*

John 3:16-17 NASB1995

Reflective Notes:

Day 16

King of Majesty

This King of majesty, Jesus Christ is He
The King of majesty, forever He shall be

He rules from heaven on high and over all below
Ensuring His elect He they'll come to know

Forever and ever the Almighty reigns
To His power, there is no restrain

There is none who can be in the presence of the Lord
Nor escape the edge of His sovereign sword

Unless he trusts Jesus for blessed salvation,
He will have from Him certain damnation

Unless He repents and trusts in the cross,

Possession of his soul, he'll suffer loss

This King of majesty is not to be trifled with
For the lake of fire is indeed no myth

For the God of the stars will torture forever
Those who reject Him, they He will sever

From all that is lovely, good, holy, and true
Except for His wrath, in which they will stew

Unending wrath, they shall endure
Having rejected the heavenly Cure

This King of majesty, Jesus is He
This King of majesty, forever He shall be

"From His mouth comes a sharp sword, so that with it He may strike down the nations, and He will rule them with a rod of iron; and He treads the wine press of the fierce wrath of God, the Almighty. And on His robe and on His thigh He has a name written, 'KING OF KINGS, AND LORD OF LORDS'."

Revelation 19:15-16 NASB1995

"which He will bring about at the proper time—He who is the blessed and only Sovereign, the King of kings and Lord of lords, who alone possesses immortality and dwells in unapproachable light, whom no one has seen or can see. To Him be honor and eternal dominion! Amen."

1 Timothy 6:15-16 NASB1995

"And being found in appearance as a man, He humbled Himself by becoming obedient to the point of death: death on a cross. For this reason also God highly exalted Him, and bestowed on Him the name which is above every name, so that at the name of Jesus every knee will bow, of those who are in heaven and on earth and under the earth, and that every tongue will confess that Jesus Christ is Lord, to the glory of God the Father."

Philippians 2:8-11 NASB1995

"Safe? Who said anything about safe? 'Course he isn't safe. But he's good. He's the King, I tell you."

-Mr. Beaver to Lucy regarding Aslan from The Lion, the Witch, and the Wardrobe by C.S. Lewis

Reflective Notes:

Day 17

<u>*Mercy*</u>

The mercy of the Lord, how sweet it is
For those who experience His lasting bliss

Though wretched we are before our very birth
His mercy saved us from the unending hearth

Those who repent of their sins and call on His name
Forever they are saved from everlasting shame

The mercy of God was displayed on the cross
To the thief and His killers to save them from loss

Has the mercy of the Lord come into your life?
Or with the God of the galaxies do you have strife?

Come and make peace with your Creator
Trust in Him as your great Savior

Believe that the mercy shown on Calvary
Was also meant for you and for me

Trust in His mercy, trust Him today
So with Him you can forever stay

The mercy of the Lord, how sweet it is
For those who experience His lasting bliss

"The Lord's acts of mercy indeed do not end, for His compassions do not fail. They are new every morning; great is Your faithfulness. 'The Lord is my portion," says my soul, 'Therefore I wait for Him.' The Lord is good to those who await Him, to the person who seeks Him. It is good that he waits silently for the salvation of the Lord."

Lamentation 3:22-26 NASB1995

"What shall we say then? There is no injustice with God, is there? May it never be! For He says to Moses, 'I will have mercy on whom I have mercy, and I will have compassion on whom I have compassion.' So then it does not depend on the man who wills or the man who runs, but on God who has mercy. For the Scripture says to Pharaoh, 'For this very purpose I raised you up, to demonstrate My power in you, and that My name might be proclaimed throughout the whole earth.' So then He has mercy on whom He desires, and He hardens

whom He desires.”

Romans 9:14-18 NASB1995

“For You, Lord, are good, and ready to forgive, and abundant in lovingkindness to all who call upon You…but You, O Lord, are a God merciful and gracious, slow to anger and abundant in lovingkindness and truth.”

Psalm 86:5, 15 NASB1995

Reflective Notes:

Day 18

Inner Gift

To the eternal King
What shall we bring?

To the Lord of the earth
Who gave us second birth?

To what will we give to He
Who rules over you and me?

Would silver and gold bring Him pleasure?
Would such delights be His treasure?

I tell you the truth, these will not due
Take heed of this, for now I warn you

To seek to please Him with mere possessions
Would indeed amount to many transgressions

Though giving such things shows our gratitude,
It should reflect our inner attitude

Not giving Him things and going on our merry way
But showing Him that we are here to stay

By giving to Him with love from our heart
In order to serve Him and do our part

For the advancement of His Gospel and His kingdom
Out of thankfulness to Him for our unending freedom

Always give to Him from the treasures of your heart
And from this solemn lesson, do not dare depart

Out of love for Him, bring forth your inner gift
Knowing that from Him, you will have no rift

Let us surrender to Him all we hold dear
And always to Him, seek to draw near

In the Savior's arms you will always be,
His inner gift for you everlastingly

"For You do not delight in sacrifice, otherwise I would give it; You are not pleased with burnt offering. The sacrifices of God are a broken spirit; a broken and a contrite heart, O God, You will not despise."

Psalm 51:16 NASB1995

"Now this I say, he who sows sparingly will also reap sparingly, and he who sows bountifully will also reap bountifully. Each one must do just as he has purposed in his heart, not grudgingly or under compulsion, for God loves a cheerful giver. And God is able to make all grace abound to you, so that always having all sufficiency in everything, you may have an abundance for every good deed; as it is written, 'He scattered abroad, he gave to the poor, His righteousness endures forever.'"

2 Corinthians 9:6-9 NASB1995

Reflective Notes:

Day 19

War

Are you ready to raise and slash with your sword
To go to war in the name of the Lord?

To fight against the god of the ages
As written on the holy pages?

To preach the Scriptures unashamed
To make His name highly proclaimed?

To preach the Gospel to all who will hear
To command them to God to indeed draw near

That their sins may be washed away
And in hopes they will learn to pray?

To speak out against evil ideals
On behalf of God to make an appeal

That they would repent of their evil mindset
And be convinced that the Scriptures are correct?

To preach against the world and its evil desires
That against the Lord they may no longer conspire?

Are you ready to sacrifice everything
In the name of the one, true, and holy King?

Will you speak the truth against those you love
While being gentle as a delicate dove?

Will you go to battle for the Lord of your life
That with Him men may no longer have any strife

In hopes they will hear and turn from their sin
And come to have the Spirit dwelling within?

Always be ready to use the Bible
In this task, never be idle

In hopes that through you
Men will know what is true

That they may repent of their sin
And forever live with Him.

"I solemnly charge you in the presence of God and of Christ Jesus, who is to judge the living and the dead, and by His appearing and His kingdom:

preach the word; be ready in season and out of season; reprove, rebuke, exhort, with great patience and instruction. But you, be sober in all things, endure hardship, do the work of an evangelist, fulfill your ministry."

2 Timothy 4:1-2, 5 NASB1995

"...but sanctify Christ as Lord in your hearts, always being ready to make a defense to everyone who asks you to give an account for the hope that is in you, yet with gentleness and reverence."

1 Peter 3:15 NASB1995

Reflective Notes:

Day 20

Firm Foundation

A firm foundation, Christ is He!
A solid rock, He'll forever be!

Through much betrayals, trials, and tribulations,
He's been with me in all my situations

Be it the storm by night or the beast by day,
He has been with me all the way

In my time of great danger
He was by no means a stranger

For many a time I have called on His name
To save me from dangerous wild game

In the night of the wild boar,
My prayer to Him did quickly soar

 "Jesus, Son of David, have mercy on me!"
For the path of the beast, I could not see

From the claw of the squirrel, he has saved my face
And saved me from scarring, physical disgrace

In the dead of the night, He met me in the woods
As I prayed for His help, as we often should

As I was desperately missing my fallen quarry,
The search for which had grown quite contrary

For in the dead of the night all looked the same
And if not careful could drive me insane

Despite my intense searching
And much repeated circling

Nothing was to be found
Which was quite profound

But after pausing to pray
The search would soon sway

For once I said amen,
The deer was found again

Praise be to the Lord, my help in time of need!
Desperate for Him, I have been indeed!

A firm foundation, Christ is He!
My solid rock, He's been for me!

Trust in Him as your rock today
Remember to Him to always pray

With repentant heart and bended knee
Submit to Him with genuine glee

Trust Him in all circumstances
He's the God of many chances

Have faith in Him through it all
And on His name, always do call

"'I love You, O Lord, my strength.' The Lord is my rock and my fortress and my deliverer, My God, my rock, in whom I take refuge; My shield and the horn of my salvation, my stronghold. I call upon the Lord, who is worthy to be praised, and I am saved from my enemies. The cords of death encompassed me, and the torrents of ungodliness terrified me. The cords of Sheol surrounded me; the snares of death confronted me. In my distress I called upon the Lord, and cried to my God for help; He heard my voice out of His temple, and my cry for help before Him came into His ears. "

Psalm 18:1-3 NASB1995

"'Therefore everyone who hears these words of Mine and acts on them, may be compared to a wise

*man who built his house on the rock. And the rain
fell, and the floods came, and the winds blew and*

*slammed against that house; and yet it did not fall,
for it had been founded on the rock. Everyone who
hears these words of Mine and does not act on them,
will be like a foolish man who built his house on the
sand. The rain fell, and the floods came, and the
winds blew and slammed against that house; and it
fell—and great was its fall.' When Jesus had
finished these words, the crowds were amazed at His
teaching; for He was teaching them as one having
authority, and not as their scribes."*

Matthew 7:24-29 NASB1995

Reflective Notes:

Day 21

Your Part

How often we sit and wait in the dark
For the Lord to give us a certain spark

Some ray of hope that we what we desire
Will come to pass and not expire

How often man will say a prayer
But lift a finger does not dare

To bring to pass his heartfelt goal
For which he yearns with all his soul

When you pray, do you take action?
Or is doing nothing your reaction?

Do you do your part as God commands?
Or do you simply trust His holy hands

With what you want with all of your being
Without the truth you might not be seeing

That you must do your part too
So that your dreams may come true

But live for the Lord in all you do
And do not dare to misconstrue

To think your dreams are better than the Lord's
But if you do, put that thought to the sword

If He wills, you shall be born again,
And repent of your many sins

Then new desires you will possess
That in your heart you will caress

With the new desires from up above
Seek them out with the Lord of love

Do your part to bring them to be
And serve Him with everlasting glee

While the Lord must be in all you do,
You must do your part too

Discover your passions from on High
And in your desires, do apply

The gifts He has given to bring Him glory
In order that you may tell His story

Of the Gospel of His Son, the great King of kings
Of whose praises His sheep shall always sing

Be it marriage, hobby, or career
Use all these things for all to hear

The message of the Lord of all
That all He chose may hear His call

In all your desires, submit to His purposes
And use them all for His divine services

Do your part to bring them about
While trusting Him to make them sprout

Though be at peace if He is not willing,
For He will always be the One, True King

Be satisfied with what you have from up above
For if you're in Him, you'll always have His love

Amen

"Make sure that your character is free from the love of money, being content with what you have; for He Himself has said, 'I will never desert you, nor will I ever forsake you,' so that we confidently say, 'The Lord is my helper, I will not be afraid. What will man do to me?'"

Hebrews 13:5-6 NASB1995

"Do not be deceived, my beloved brethren. Every good thing given and every perfect gift is from above, coming down from the Father of lights, with whom there is no variation or shifting shadow."

James 1:16-17 NASB1995

"Whatever you do in word or deed, do all in the name of the Lord Jesus, giving thanks through Him to God the Father."

Colossians 3:17 NASB1995

Reflective Notes:

Day 22

<u>Weary</u>

Are you weary from life's battles?
Will you soon fall off the saddle?

Does all seem hopeless on this ride?
Is there no one by your side?

Does it seem that life is full of dread?
Are you hanging on by just a thread?

Though it all may seem dark and grim
And a chance of hope seems mighty slim

Put your hope in the Father above
And trust in His lasting love

No matter how dark your weighty plight
Strive to keep Him in your sight

Always remember not all is lost
Due to Him who paid the cost

He has the final say in all you do
His faithfulness indeed is true

Rely on Him for strength in the fight
And always to Him forever hold tight

From those who are His, He'll never leave
So be sure to Christ to forever cleave

Rest on His every promise your anxious heart
Never from His word do you dare depart

When in the battle, use His mighty sword
And always remember, the results are of the Lord

"Come to Me, all who are weary and heavy-laden, and I will give you rest. Take My yoke upon you and learn from Me, for I am gentle and humble in heart, and YOU WILL FIND REST FOR YOUR SOULS. For My yoke is easy and My burden is light."

Matthew 11:28-30 NASB1995

"Therefore humble yourselves under the mighty hand of God, that He may exalt you at the proper time, casting all your anxiety on Him, because He cares for you."

1 Peter 5:6-7 NASB1995

"Lift up your heads, O gates, and be lifted up, O ancient doors, that the King of glory may come in! Who is the King of glory? The Lord strong and mighty, the Lord mighty in battle. Lift up your heads, O gates, And lift them up, O ancient doors, That the King of glory may come in! Who is this King of glory? The Lord of hosts, He is the King of glory. Selah."

Psalm 24:7-10 NASB1995

Reflective Notes:

Day 23

Fallen

Though once they were new and young
Way back when when spring had sprung

In this day they are dead and brown
As a result, they have come down

Fallen they are from their former glory
Bringing an end to their short-lived story

So it is too with all mankind
Whose former glory was left behind

Fallen is he because of his sin
But through the Spirit can be born again

A new creation he will always be
For all mankind to truly see

That the Lord has made a wretch His treasure
Whom He has changed both now and forever

Have you my friend been born again?
Have you truly looked deep within?

Have you been saved by God's grace
To forever be in His warm embrace?

Have you been changed within your person
To where you have a new assertion

Against the sin in which you partake?
From it now do you flee and forsake?

Do you now desire the things of heaven
And fight against all worldly leaven?

Do you desire to call men to repent
And proclaim He who is heaven-sent?

Do you have newfound love for your enemy
That by all in your life is plain to see?

Do you desire to proclaim the Gospel to all men
That they may know Jesus and repent of their sin?

Have you been changed from the inside out
To where it is He whom you are about?

Do you bear the heavenly fruits of the Holy Spirit?
Do you proclaim the Gospel to all who will hear it?

If you have no change, you have no Christ
If this is you, then be contrite

For you are fallen because of your sin
And assuredly have no Christ within

If for your many sins you are convicted
And yearn for Christ who was lifted

Repent of your sins and trust in Him today
New birth you'll be given and in Him forever stay

Then live for Jesus the rest of your days
Until you go home and sing His praise

Then continue to serve Him throughout eternity
As you cherish each other with unending glee

"...for all have sinned and fall short of the glory of God..."

Romans 3:23 NASB1995

"But now having been freed from sin and enslaved to God, you derive your benefit, resulting in sanctification, and the outcome, eternal life. For the wages of sin is death, but the free gift of God is eternal life in Christ Jesus our Lord."

Romans 6:22-23 NASB1995

"Therefore if anyone is in Christ, he is a new creature; the old things passed away; behold, new things have come."

2 Corinthians 5:17 NASB1995

"Jesus answered and said to him, 'Truly, truly, I say to you, unless one is born again he cannot see the kingdom of God.' Nicodemus said to Him, 'How can a man be born when he is old? He cannot enter a second time into his mother's womb and be born, can he?' Jesus answered, 'Truly, truly, I say to you, unless one is born of water and the Spirit he cannot enter into the kingdom of God. That which is born of the flesh is flesh, and that which is born of the Spirit is spirit. Do not be amazed that I said to you, 'You must be born again.' The wind blows where it wishes and you hear the sound of it, but do not know where it comes from and where it is going; so is everyone who is born of the Spirit.'"

John 3:3-9 NASB1995

"Blessed be the God and Father of our Lord Jesus Christ, who according to His great mercy has caused us to be born again to a living hope through the resurrection of Jesus Christ from the dead..."

1 Peter 1:3 NASB1995

"But if you are led by the Spirit, you are not under the Law. Now the deeds of the flesh are evident, which are: immorality, impurity, sensuality, idolatry,

sorcery, enmities, strife, jealousy, outbursts of anger, disputes, dissensions, factions, envying, drunkenness, carousing, and things like these, of which I forewarn you, just as I have forewarned you, that those who practice such things will not inherit the kingdom of God. But the fruit of the Spirit is love, joy, peace, patience, kindness, goodness, faithfulness, gentleness, self-control; against such things there is no law. Now those who belong to Christ Jesus have crucified the flesh with its passions and desires. If we live by the Spirit, let us also walk by the Spirit."

Galatians 5:18-25 NASB1995

Reflective Notes:

Day 24

<u>Sword of Discipline</u>

The discipline of the Lord
How painful is that sword

Everywhere it seems to be
From its presence you cannot flee

In whatever sin you fight
This sword will be your plight

Though this sword is very good
It can be quite misunderstood

Though this sword is extremely painful
For its blade you will be grateful

Its cutting edge will make you humble

So that in pride you will not stumble

It will make you like Jesus Christ
So in your sin you'll be contrite

In the Lord always strive to stay
Never again from Him to sway

When you are stabbed by the Lord
And are disciplined by the sword

Recall it is the blade of love
That you may be gentle as a dove

In order that we may shine His light for all to see
That those who look may know Him with glee

For if we are to live for the Lord
We must endure His holy sword

Remember though that you are forgiven
And a new heart you have been given

Live for the Lord in all you do
And no matter what, He always loves you

"'My son, do not regard lightly the discipline of the Lord, nor faint when you are reproved by Him; For those whom the Lord loves He disciplines, and He scourges every son whom He receives.' It is for discipline that you endure; God deals with you as with sons; for what son is there whom his father does not discipline? But if you are without

discipline, of which all have become partakers, then you are illegitimate children and not sons.

Furthermore, we had earthly fathers to discipline us, and we respected them; shall we not much rather be subject to the Father of spirits, and live? For they disciplined us for a short time as seemed best to them, but He disciplines us for our good, so that we may share His holiness. All discipline for the moment seems not to be joyful, but sorrowful; yet to those who have been trained by it, afterwards it yields the peaceful fruit of righteousness."

Hebrews 12:5b-11

Reflective Notes:

<u>The Love of God</u>

The love of God who can understand
That He would save us by His hand?

How is it He could love you and me
And receive us with unending glee?

That He would slaughter His Son upon the cross
So that you and I would not be at loss

So that we could be in heaven with Him
And have His Holy Spirit dwell within?

To become a part of His family
So that all may hear and see

His great love and amazing grace
So we can forever behold His face

To stand in the presence of the Lord above
Who saved His children by His great love

Never shall they be tortured in the lake of fire
With those who against Him they did conspire

For they trusted in the Risen One
Who over sin and death has won

In His love we will always be
Now and throughout eternity

Praise God for His unending love
Who is as gentle as a dove

Because of His love, we will always have freedom
In the land of paradise, His everlasting kingdom

For the love of God has set us free
And with Him we will always be

The love of God who can understand
That He would save us by His hand?

How is it He could love you and me
And receive us with unending glee?

"Shout for joy, O daughter of Zion! Shout in triumph, O Israel! Rejoice and exult with all your heart, O daughter of Jerusalem! The Lord has taken away His judgments against you, He has cleared away your enemies. The King of Israel, the Lord, is in your midst; You will fear disaster no more. In that day it will be said to Jerusalem: 'Do not be afraid, O Zion; Do not let your hands fall limp. 'The Lord your God is in your midst, a victorious warrior. He will exult over you with joy, He will be quiet in His love, He will rejoice over you with shouts of joy.'"

Zephaniah 3:14-17 NASB1995

Reflective Notes:

Day 26

The Holiness of God

The holiness of God is to be feared
And will one day by all be revered

The holiness of God is to be praised
For by it His Son was forever raised

The holiness of God is seen by all men
Whether or not they're born again

The holiness of God is observed in all creation
And will give all men a great sensation

The holiness of God is awesome in all its splendor
And is glorious in all its many wonders

The holiness of God causes men to perish forever
For because of their sin, from Him they are severed

The holiness of God blesses His chosen ones
For it is for them the victory has been won

The holiness of God drove Christ to the cross
So that His children would not be a loss

The holiness of God brought payment for our sin
So that by His grace we could be born again

The holiness of God brought His elect everlasting life
So that forever they could cease from all painful strife

The holiness of God is great indeed
Forever which will never recede

"The heavens are telling of the glory of God; and their expanse is declaring the work of His hands. Day to day pours forth speech, and night to night reveals knowledge. There is no speech, nor are there words; their voice is not heard. Their line has gone out through all the earth, and their utterances to the end of the world. In them He has placed a tent for the sun, which is as a bridegroom coming out of his chamber; it rejoices as a strong man to run his course. Its rising is from one end of the heavens, and its circuit to the other end of them; and there is nothing hidden from its heat."

Psalm 19:1-6 NASB1995

"'Cease striving and know that I am God; I will be exalted among the nations, I will be exalted in the earth.' The Lord of hosts is with us; the God of Jacob is our stronghold. Selah."

Psalm 46:10-11 NASB1995

"I will magnify Myself, sanctify Myself, and make Myself known in the sight of many nations; and they will know that I am the Lord."

Ezekiel 38:23 NASB1995

Reflective Notes:

Day 27

___Light of the World___

The light of the world is on display
So that from sin man may sway

It is a gift given from above
Coming down with heavenly love

The Light of the world was slain on a tree
So the light of the world the elect could see

The light of the world is seen through good deeds
That those of the world might see Him indeed

Through love and good works it can be shown
So that the love of Christ might be known

Gentleness and kindness are of it too

So that the light may be seen as true

By those who don't know the Lord
That they may escape His sword

Are you a bearer of the light?
Do you participate in the fight

Against the darkness of the earth
Along with those of second birth?

Shine His light in all you do
So they might know He is true

Proclaim the Gospel; call men to repent
Shine the light that is heaven-sent

"You are the light of the world. A city set on a hill cannot be hidden; nor does anyone light a lamp and put it under a basket, but on the lampstand, and it gives light to all who are in the house. Let your light shine before men in such a way that they may see your good works, and glorify your Father who is in heaven."

Matthew 5:14-16 NASB1995

"Then Jesus again spoke to them, saying, 'I am the Light of the world; he who follows Me will not walk in the darkness, but will have the Light of life.'"

John 8:12 NASB1995

*"Then the King will say to those on His right,
'Come, you who are blessed of My Father, inherit
the kingdom prepared for you from the foundation
of the world. For I was hungry, and you gave Me
something to eat; I was thirsty, and you gave Me
something to drink; I was a stranger, and you
invited Me in; naked, and you clothed Me; I was
sick, and you visited Me; I was in prison, and you
came to Me.'"*

Matthew 25:34-36 NASB1995

Reflective Notes:

Day 28

Grace

The grace of God is water of love
Forever flowing from above

Never will His grace run out
From heaven's gracious water spout

His grace is endless, yes indeed
This grace is endless for you and me

For His chosen ones, they have His grace
Always and forever, they'll behold His face

For those who repent of their sin
In whom He lives within

Who trust in Him for blessed salvation
Believing Him to be their propitiation

For them the grace of God will be
For now and throughout eternity

Let us go and sin no more,
For by His grace He made us soar

In freedom from all our sin
And made us born again

Now go tell people of the grace of Christ
That they may repent and not be contrite

For the grace of God is water of love
Forever flowing from above

Never will His grace run out
From heaven's gracious water spout

His grace is endless, yes indeed
His grace is endless for you and me

*"For by grace you have been saved through faith;
and that not of yourselves, it is the gift of God; not
as a result of works, so that no one may boast."*

Ephesians 2:8-9 NASB1995

"…being justified as a gift by His grace through the redemption which is in Christ Jesus…"

Romans 3:24 NASB1995

"But the free gift is not like the transgression. For if by the transgression of the one the many died, much more did the grace of God and the gift by the grace of the one Man, Jesus Christ, abound to the many."

Romans 5:15 NASB1995

"But if it is by grace, it is no longer on the basis of works, otherwise grace is no longer grace."

Romans 6:11 NASB1995

Reflective Notes:

Day 29

<u>Memories</u>

Memories new and memories old
Many of which are solid gold

Some in which time stood still
And were pleasant as a daffodil

That are sweet to the soul and precious to the heart
Shared with those who we wish to not depart

However much we want them not to leave
And desperately want to always cleave

The sad truth is this cannot be
Unless we see them in eternity

Only through Christ can we be together
With those we love, both now and forever

In the land in which byes are never lasting
Because their lives are everlasting

Those whom we love here on the earth
We want not to see in the everlasting hearth

Precious memories we have with them in this life
And more we desire to in the land of no strife

So call them to repent and proclaim the Gospel today
And for their salvation never cease to pray

In hopes with them you can make
And forevermore appreciate

Memories new and memories old
All of which would be solid gold

*"Then I saw a new heaven and a new earth; for the
first heaven and the first earth passed away, and
there is no longer any sea. And I saw the holy city,
new Jerusalem, coming down out of heaven from
God, made ready as a bride adorned for her
husband. And I heard a loud voice from the throne,
saying, 'Behold, the tabernacle of God is among
men, and He will dwell among them, and they shall
be His people, and God Himself will be among them
and He will wipe away every tear from their eyes;
and there will no longer be any death; there will no
longer be any mourning, or crying, or pain; the first*

things have passed away.' And He who sits on the throne said, 'Behold, I am making all things new.' And He said, 'Write, for these words are faithful and true.'"

Revelation 21:1-5 NASB1995

"I say to you that many will come from east and west, and recline at the table with Abraham, Isaac, and Jacob in the kingdom of heaven; but the sons of the kingdom will be cast out into the outer darkness; in that place there will be weeping and gnashing of teeth."

John 8:11-12 NASB1995

"But for the cowardly and unbelieving and abominable and murderers and immoral persons and sorcerers and idolaters and all liars, their part will be in the lake that burns with fire and brimstone, which is the second death."

Revelation 21:8 NASB1995

"Blessed are those who wash their robes, so that they may have the right to the tree of life, and may enter by the gates into the city. Outside are the dogs and the sorcerers and the immoral persons and the murderers and the idolaters, and everyone who loves and practices lying."

Revelation 22:14-15 NASB1995

Reflective Notes:

Day 30

<u>*Safe*</u>

Safe in the arms of Christ
Who willingly paid the price

For the safety of our everlasting souls
By through His body taking on the tolls

Of the weight of our great sin
So we would be born again

To receive everlasting salvation
And escape certain damnation

In Him our lives will always be
Safe here and throughout eternity

So while on earth, you have no need to fear
Because of Him who is always so near

You will always be safe in His arms
So there is no need for any alarm

No matter what troubles come your way
Let your faith in Him never sway

Since you trust Him with what you cannot see
Can you not trust Him earnestly

In the here and now with what is seen
Yet in the hands of the unseen King?

For in the arms of the Sheperd you'll always be
Both now and forever, throughout eternity

"He who dwells in the shelter of the Most High Will abide in the shadow of the Almighty. I will say to the LORD, 'My refuge and my fortress, My God, in whom I trust!' For it is He who delivers you from the snare of the trapper and from the deadly pestilence. He will cover you with His pinions, and under His wings you may seek refuge; His faithfulness is a shield and bulwark."

Psalm 91:1-4 NASB1995

"I sought the Lord, and He answered me, and delivered me from all my fears. They looked to Him and were radiant, and their faces will never be ashamed. This poor man cried, and the Lord heard him and saved him out of all his troubles. The angel of the Lord encamps around those who fear Him,

and rescues them."

Psalm 34:4-7 NASB1995

"But now, thus says the Lord, your Creator, O Jacob, and He who formed you, O Israel, 'Do not fear, for I have redeemed you; I have called you by name; you are Mine! When you pass through the waters, I will be with you; and through the rivers, they will not overflow you. when you walk through the fire, you will not be scorched, nor will the flame burn you."

Isaiah 43:1-3 NASB1995

"The Lord is my shepherd, I shall not want. He makes me lie down in green pastures; He leads me beside quiet waters. He restores my soul; He guides me in the paths of righteousness for His name's sake. Even though I walk through the valley of the shadow of death, I fear no evil, for You are with me; Your rod and Your staff, they comfort me. You prepare a table before me in the presence of my enemies; You have anointed my head with oil; my cup overflows. Surely goodness and lovingkindness will follow me all the days of my life, and I will dwell in the house of the Lord forever."

Psalm 23:1-6 NASB1995

"Truly, truly, I say to you, he who hears My word, and believes Him who sent Me, has eternal life, and does not come into judgment, but has passed out of

death into life."

John 5:24 NASB1995

"Jesus said to her, 'I am the resurrection and the life; he who believes in Me will live even if he dies, and everyone who lives and believes in Me will never die. Do you believe this?' She said to Him, 'Yes, Lord; I have believed that You are the Christ, the Son of God, even He who comes into the world.'"

John 11:25-27 NASB1995

"Safe? Who said anything about safe? 'Course he isn't safe. But he's good. He's the King, I tell you."

-Mr. Beaver to Lucy regarding Aslan from The Lion, the Witch, and the Wardrobe by C.S. Lewis

Reflective Notes:

Day 31

<u>*Forgiven*</u>

Forgiven I am, with lasting salvation
Because of Him, my one propitiation

For the shed blood took away my sin
Now and forever, I will be with Him

Where are my sins? They have gone missing!
Because of His blood, in which I was rinsing

Washed in His blood I have been
Forever gone is my dreadful sin

Every sin I have committed
Has forever been omitted

Because of He who took my place
I shall forever behold His face

To always be with He who forgives
By His grace, I'll forever live

In His presence with saints alike
Never again to be contrite

For I am forgiven through the blood of the Lamb
Through He who is the Great I Am

This I promise to you
You can be forgiven too

Repent of your sins and trust in Him today
Submit your life to Him and never from Him sway

Put faith in Him who died on the cross
So you will not be a lasting loss

So it can be said of you
That no matter what you do,

"Forgiven I am, with lasting salvation
Because of Him, my one propitiation

For the shed blood took away my sin
Now and forever, I will be with Him!"

"but if we walk in the Light as He Himself is in the Light, we have fellowship with one another, and the blood of Jesus His Son cleanses us from all sin. If

*we say that we have no sin, we are deceiving
ourselves and the truth is not in us. If we confess
our sins, He is faithful and righteous to forgive us
our sins and to cleanse us from all unrighteousness.
If we say that we have not sinned, we make Him a
liar and His word is not in us."*

1 John 1:7-10 NASB1995

*"Therefore there is now no condemnation for those
who are in Christ Jesus. For the law of the Spirit of
life in Christ Jesus has set you free from the law of
sin and of death."*

Romans 8:1-2 NASB1995

Reflective Notes:

<u>Conclusion</u>

My dear reader, thank you for your time and energy in reading these numerous poems. I hope and pray that the Lord will use them to grow you, strengthen you, and perhaps even save you. Though this poetry book covers a variety of topics, remember that above all we are to bring glory to God in all we do, proclaim the Gospel, and submit every area of our lives to Him.

There is a vast world out there that needs the Lord Jesus Christ, and though you cannot reach everyone in this world unless He wills that to be, you can reach those who are in your world. Who is it that you know that does not know our Lord and Savior Jesus Christ? Your spouse? Your children? Your family? Your friends? How about your boss, co-workers, and acquaintances? There are likely even people at your own church who do not know the Lord.

Those who do not know Christ will everlastingly

suffer in the lake of fire to be eaten on by worms, burned alive, and have their spines bent while thirsting in darkness and isolation throughout an endless eternity. There is much here to be concerned about. Out of love for those who are in our lives, let us proclaim the Gospel to them and call them to Christ and to repentance, before it is too late and they are forever damned to experience such horrible fates.

Remember, no matter how hard this life gets, always recall the hope we have in heaven, and let everything you do be done in light of this blazing bright hope. In your darkest of days, in your most private of moments, when all seems lost with no way out, do not lose hope, regardless of how dark the storm. No matter how bleak your situation may seem, know that "…God causes all things to work together for good to those who love God, to those who are called according to His purpose," (Romans 8:28). Aside from the glory of God, your sanctification, and putting you in a dark situation so that others may see the light of Christ shine through you in your troubled times, the reasons for why certain things happen to you we might not ever know until we are with Him.

Hold on to Him. Hold on to His many promises. Hold on to His truth. Hold on to the Lord Jesus Christ in everything that happens in your life and in every circumstance in which you find yourself. For those who are His, there is always hope. There is always a brighter future. Not always for our life here on this earth, but the things that happen here can affect what happens to us in the next life. Not in regard to losing salvation (which is not possible in accordance to John 10:27-29), but in terms of rewards, placement, and us for eternity living with how we lived here on earth.

More importantly though, the things that occur to us in this life God will use for His glory, your everlasting good, and the advancement of His Gospel and His kingdom. Aside from the three aforementioned reasons, we do not always know why but God willing we will know at some point after we see Him. Whatever occurs to you, trust Him with all you have and all you are. Live for Him, to the very end. No matter what. If you are His, I'll see you there.

"You therefore, my son, be strong in the grace that is in Christ Jesus. The things which you have heard from me in the presence of many witnesses, entrust these to faithful men who will be able to teach others also. Suffer hardship with me, as a good soldier of Christ Jesus. No soldier in active service entangles himself in the affairs of everyday life, so that he may please the one who enlisted him as a soldier. Also if anyone competes as an athlete, he does not win the prize unless he competes according to the rules. The hard-working farmer ought to be the first to receive his share of the crops. Consider what I say, for the Lord will give you understanding in everything.

Remember Jesus Christ, risen from the dead descendant of David, according to my gospel, for which I suffer hardship even to imprisonment as a criminal; but the Word of God is not imprisoned.

For this reason I endure all things for the sake of those who are chosen, so that they also may obtain the salvation which is in Christ Jesus and with it eternal glory. It is a trustworthy statement: for if we died with Him, we will also live with Him; if we endure, we will also reign with Him; if we deny Him, He also will deny us; if we are faithless, He remains faithful, for He cannot deny Himself.

2 Timothy 2:1-13 NASB1995

"I solemnly charge you in the presence of God and of Christ Jesus, who is to judge the living and the dead and by His appearing and His kingdom: preach the word; be ready in season and out of season; reprove, rebuke, exhort, with great patience and instruction. For the time will come when they will not endure sound doctrine; but wanting to have their ears tickled, they will accumulate for themselves teachers in accordance to their own desires, and will turn away their ears from the truth and will turn aside to myths. But you, be sober in all things, endure hardship, do the work of an evangelist, fulfill your ministry.

For I am already being poured out as a drink offering, and the time of my departure has come. I have fought the good fight, I have finished the course, I have kept the faith; in the future there is laid up for me the crown of righteousness, which the Lord, the righteous Judge, will award to me on that day; and not only to me, but also to all who have loved His appearing."

---

2 Timothy 4:1-9 NASB1995

"Therefore, since we have so great a cloud of witnesses surrounding us, let us also lay aside every encumbrance and the sin which so easily entangles us, and let us run with endurance the race that is set before us, fixing our eyes on Jesus, the author and perfecter of faith, who for the joy set before Him endured the cross, despising the shame, and has sat down at the right hand of the throne of God. For consider Him who endured such hostility by sinners against Himself, so that you will not grow weary and lose heart."

Hebrews 12:1-4 NASB1995

"Not that I have already obtained it or have already become perfect, but I press on so that I may lay hold of that for which also I was laid hold of by Christ Jesus. Brethren, I do not regard myself as having laid hold of it yet; but one thing I do: forgetting what lies behind and reaching forward to what lies ahead, I press on toward the goal for the prize of the upward call of God in Christ Jesus. Let us therefore, as many as are perfect, have this attitude; and if in anything you have a different attitude, God will reveal that also to you; however, let us keep living by that same standard to which we have attained."

Philippians 3:12-16 NASB1995

"But the eleven disciples proceeded to Galilee, to the

mountain which Jesus had designated. When they saw Him, they worshiped Him; but some were doubtful. And Jesus came up and spoke to them, saying, 'All authority has been given to Me in heaven and on earth. Go therefore and make disciples of all the nations, baptizing them in the name of the Father and the Son and the Holy Spirit, teaching them to observe all that I commanded you; and lo, I am with you always, even to the end of the age.'"

Matthew 28:16-20 NASB1995

Stay in Touch

Greetings, dear reader! Thank you for reading the many poems of this book. If you desire to reach out to me, you may do so at reformedpoet398@gmail.com. Whether it be questions or concerns you may have, or requests such as speaking engagements, desiring a signed copy, or anything else that may be on your mind, you may email me, message me through my personal Facebook page, or message me through my any of the social media platforms listed after this.

Thank you again for reading this book. May the Lord guide you on your journey and carry you through all trials and tribulations. Remember that when all seems dark and hopeless, in your darkest hour, in your most private of moments, there is always the light of hope that is found in the one star that always shines brightly no matter the storm, the Bright and Morning

Star, the Lord Jesus Christ, the Son of Almighty God.

Cling to Him and surrender to Him. Repent of all your sins, submit your life to Him out of love for Him and not out of mere obligation, have faith that His suffering on and before the cross and His death on the cross paid the price for your sins, confess Him as Lord, and believe in your heart that God raised Him from the dead. Do all these things with a genuine heart, and you will be saved. Then walk with confidence that as you put Him first in all you do, He will always take care of you. If you are His adopted chosen child, He will always be with you, both now and throughout the rest of eternity, no matter what.

Social Media Platforms:

Email: reformedpoet398@gmail.com

YouTube: Poems for the Christian Heart

Facebook: Poems for the Christian Heart

Tik Tok: @poemsfortheChrist

Instagram: poemsforthechristianheart

X (formely known as Twitter): PoemsfortheChristianHeart/@poemsforchrist

www.ingramcontent.com/pod-product-compliance
Lightning Source LLC
Chambersburg PA
CBHW031410150726
47989CB00002B/598

9798892694100